CONTENTS

PREFACE

People come to speaking coaches like me for a variety of reasons. Some are looking for a stronger connection with an audience. Some want to be more persuasive. Some want help with delivery techniques.

But almost all of them want one thing: to have more confidence as a speaker. "What would that look like?" I ask them. Their answers run the gamut:

"I wouldn't have sweaty palms, a dry mouth, and a tight throat."

"I wouldn't feel stressed and sleep-deprived as my presentation approaches."

"I would know without a doubt that my story could make a difference."

"I wouldn't feel like an impostor the minute I'm on the stage."

"I would feel calm and relaxed, knowing I deserve to be up there."

What I have learned from these conversations is that there is no single approach to building confidence and overcoming anxiety when it comes to public speaking. People talk of overcoming "fear of public speaking" as if *fear* were all there is to it. But I have found the emotions around public speaking to be more complex than that. Yes, fear is real: fear of failure, fear of public embarrassment, fear that one's message won't turn out to be helpful to the audience. But feelings of unworthiness are also in play, couched in the thought "Who am I to stand up there and tell my story?" or "When I have to present this report, I'll do such a bad job that they'll figure out I'm not as smart as they thought."

That is why this book takes a multi-pronged approach to helping you build confidence and calm your nerves when it is your turn to speak. It is not enough, in my view, to give you tips for dealing with dry mouth and other symptoms without also helping you get to the root of your speaking anxiety.

For many speakers, that anxiety is rooted in doubts about their self-worth and the value of their message, so we tackle that right away in Chapter 1. Another source of anxiety I have seen is for a speaker to be too focused on himself or herself and not on their audience and what the audience stands to gain from hearing the message. We will address that in Chapter 2. Is your anxiety caused by lack of preparation? See Chapter 3 for tips on the most effective ways to prepare.

When you finish the first three chapters, I predict you will find your confidence increasing and your anxiety decreasing. Yet you may still have symptoms of public-speaking anxiety and want to know how to deal with them. You will find practical tips and tricks of the trade in Chapter 4.

Chapters 5 and 6 are more specialized. Chapter 5 addresses the case of speaking to a high-status audience, such as when a middle manager presents a report to her company's CEO and other "C-level" executives, or perhaps even the Board of Directors. Chapter 6 answers this question: "What if this speech (or sermon, or eulogy) gets me choked up emotionally?" Yes, that does happen. And yes, there are some tips that will help you get past it.

The book concludes with Chapter 7. "Go for connection, not perfection." In fact, that statement could be considered the theme of the whole book. The more you learn to set your ego aside and seek a genuine connection with your audience, the more satisfying your speaking experience will be. And your confidence will build with every satisfying experience.

CHAPTER 1

Your message has value

"Don't let fear, perfectionism, and wanting to be liked stand in the way from sharing your message."

ROBYN CONLEY DOWNS

I once had the privilege of coaching a woman who was to be the featured speaker at a fundraising dinner. The beneficiary of the fundraiser was an organization that offered shelter to women escaping abusive relationships. The speaker—I'll call her Linda—was a survivor of such a relationship. She had a powerful story to tell. But she was not ready to tell it, and thus she came to me.

Before I continue, here's a caveat. This chapter might not apply to you if the content of your speech is purely business or technical information, with no personal story involved. If that is the case, and you are already convinced you are the best person to deliver that information, then feel free to move on to Chapter 2. But if you have any doubt about your worthiness to take the stage, read on.

Back to Linda. The message I got from her initially was "I'm not sure my story will be any help to others."

She said this despite having moved clear across the country to get away from her abuser. "Lots of women have been through what I went through. Who am I to tell my story and think it has value?"

"Well, who are you *not* to?" I replied.

Your story deserves to be told

My point to Linda was that if she withheld her story, she might be denying someone else the opportunity to hear it and be moved to action. Statistically, there was a significant likelihood that out of the hundred people expected to attend the dinner, some number of them—most likely, but not necessarily, women—would be in the type of emotionally and economically abusive situation she had escaped. And wouldn't she want them to know they could escape as well?

"Who am I to think anyone would want to hear *my* story?" is a common refrain among struggling speakers. I used to think that was selfishness disguised as false modesty. But through further reading and study, I came to recognize it as a form of self-protection. When your subconscious mind tries to keep you from doing something—whether it's speaking to an audience or jumping out of an airplane—it is trying to keep you safe.

Your brain is designed to do two things: keep you alive and conserve energy. The whole jumping-out-of-airplanes thing appears to threaten the first goal, so your mind raises all kinds of objections, which a skydiving instructor must overcome. I doubt anyone seriously believes that sharing their story with an audience is a threat to their continued existence. And yet, it *is* threatening in its own way. We all share a primal need for connection with others in our tribe, for that connection was once essential to our survival. What do we truly fear when we speak? We fear rejection by our tribe. Humiliation. Expulsion. Disconnection.

Against that backdrop, convincing ourselves that sharing our story will actually *help* our tribe requires effort. Energy. And remember, our brain is programmed to conserve energy. Wouldn't it be easier to let someone else get up and tell a story? Someone the tribe won't reject, like the wise elder who holds all our stories?

So our self-preservation instinct kicks in and tries to stop us: "Who am I to think anyone would want to hear *my* story?" That inner voice is the voice of self-protection. And the way to overcome it is to think not of being banished from your tribe but of failing to help them. In a sense, you *owe* your audience your story. Your personal story of overcoming a significant obstacle in your life has the potential to help someone else see how to remove their own obstacle. Sharing your story is an act of generosity.

Further, it's not just an altruistic matter of desiring to help others that is at stake here. It is also a question of learning to inhabit your own uniqueness. There is only one you in the world. That means you are the only person who can tell this story, because it is not the tribal elder's story to tell—it's yours. Your story is valuable because *you* are valuable.

Fortunately, I was able to convince Linda of this truth, and we went on to shape what turned out to be a powerful speech that boosted the shelter's fundraising efforts. She was later asked to serve on the board of that organization and ended up chairing the next year's event. Therefore, at least one life was changed by her willingness to speak up.

What did it take to bring about this change in Linda's thinking? How were we able to boost her confidence to the point that she could prepare and deliver her message?

To be clear, Linda deserves the lion's share of the credit. By the time she came to me, she had already done the hard, emotional work of recovering from the abuse and rebuilding her life. Although she had doubts about giving a speech, she was a strong and confident woman. Still, before she could move ahead with the speech, it took my helping her see that (a) her message had value to others, and (b) no one else could tell it as powerfully as she could.

What does this mean for you? It means that your inner voice saying "Who am I to speak?" is not allowed to have the last word. To silence that voice, it might help to figure out where it is coming from. Was there a time when you did speak up and were harshly criticized for it? If there was a specific incident when that happened, try to bring it to mind. Can you identify who your critic was? Will that person be present in your audience? Probably not, I'll venture to say. Knowing that, how can you begin to let go of that critical message? Linda later told me, "I had to own it," meaning she had to take personal responsibility for her emotional response to the prospect of sharing her story. What personal work do you need to do to own your story and to wrestle it away from that inner voice?

Remember, you are not jumping out of an airplane. What your brain is trying to protect you from is *temporary* embarrassment, not permanent rejection. The first step in silencing that negative inner voice is to recognize that it is a form of self-protection, but what it is trying to protect you from is *not* a threat to your existence.

Your story has value for others

The second step in silencing that negative voice is to replace it with one carrying a different message: "Others in my tribe deserve to benefit from what I learned." This thought begins to shift your thinking from yourself to your audience (a topic we will deal with in more depth in the next chapter). Being audience-focused is an important practice for any speaker to develop. To this day, before I go in front of an audience, I ask myself, "What do they stand to gain from hearing me?" In my coaching, I have found that many speakers have yet to develop this practice.

To overcome that protective inner voice, you must focus on your listeners' needs more than your own. This will be easier if you approach a speaking opportunity with a sincere desire to help others. Remember, your job as a speaker is not to improve your own emotional outlook by telling your story (therapy is the tool for that!) but rather to improve your audience's condition. What do you want your listeners to think, do, or feel differently after hearing you speak? That is your specific purpose. How does your story support that specific purpose? It can do so by showing the change that came about in your life as you overcame your obstacle.

(If you want to know *how* to tell your story so that this change is evident to others, I suggest you read the first book in this series, *The Speaker's Quick Guide to Telling Better Stories: Connect with Any Audience and Deliver a More Meaningful, Memorable Message.*)

Your story is unique; its message is universal

"But," you may be wondering, "how can my story help others when the circumstances of it are unique to me? Won't it help only those people who are experiencing the same thing I did?"

This self-limiting thought is yet another instance of your inner voice trying to protect you and keep you comfortable by devaluing your experience. Every story has elements that are unique to the circumstances and characters being described. Yet every good story also has elements that are universal, no matter how unique the details.

Consider something as simple as Aesop's fable about the fox and the grapes. The fox is wandering through a vineyard and sees grapes he wants, but they are hanging out of his reach. After many attempts at getting to them, he gives up and slinks away, muttering, "They were probably sour grapes anyway." Moral: We tend to disparage what we cannot have.

The moral indicates that there is a universal theme present in the story's specifics. What was the fox striving for? To get the grapes. Must the reader of the fable desire a bunch of grapes to learn something from this story? Of course not! At some point, we all desire something that is beyond our reach. The desire is simultaneously specific and universal.

To see the value of your story, then, you must first identify the specific thing you want, and then you must ask yourself how it might represent a universal desire that your listeners will share. Similarly, once you identify what obstacle you had to overcome and how you did so, ask yourself what lesson others can take away from hearing what you did.

In other words, you ask four questions:

1. What were you striving for?
2. What related desire is someone else you know striving for?
3. What did you learn that helped you remove the obstacle to your striving?
4. What can someone else learn from this?

Return to Linda one more time. What was she striving for? A way out of a relationship that left her feeling devalued, as well as an escape from the economic straitjacket imposed on her by her abuser. What is everyone striving for? A way to improve their condition despite feeling trapped by circumstances. This is a more universal expression of Linda's specific situation.

And what did Linda learn? "That I had the strength to be on my own," she told me. "There comes a point when you have to realize how strong you are." What can others learn from this? That they can summon their own strength to change once they are ready to say, "Enough is enough."

Use these four questions to reveal to yourself the value of your story. Telling your story to others, when you sincerely desire to improve their condition, takes courage and selflessness. It is not an act of self-aggrandizement. It is an act of generosity. Your story is a gift only you can give. When your inner voice tries to tell you otherwise, ask yourself what it is trying to protect you from. Then remember that your tribe—your audience—wants you to succeed. They do not want to shun you; otherwise, they would not be there to hear you. Listen to that voice of self-protection but don't be ruled by it. Draw upon the lessons of this chapter to overrule it, then strap on your parachute!

Fittingly, I will give Linda the final word:

"Now I understand that my story matters."

CHAPTER 2

Focus on your audience, not yourself

"Your life is controlled by what you focus on."

—TONY ROBBINS

In 2015, I helped judge a collegiate speech contest. The reason I remember that event specifically is a memorable student I met there named Rodrigo, from Brazil. After doing well in the contest, Rodrigo approached me to ask for help with his speaking. "I already have done a lot of public speaking in my own country," he said. "But it is still a struggle for me. I thought it would get easier as I kept doing it, but still I get very nervous. Do you have any advice for me?"

Usually, my first advice for any nervous speaker is to practice, practice, practice—preferably in front of an audience such as a Toastmasters club. Rodrigo appeared practiced enough to win a speech contest, but still his nerves were getting to him. So I moved to the next suggestion. I said, "Try looking at your speech from the audience's point of view. Instead of thinking of it as a performance you put on, think about what the audience needs from you most. How will your message make a difference to them?"

Rodrigo struck me as a young man concerned about making a good impression. By my estimation, he was putting his need to look good ahead of his listeners' needs. He was also putting himself and his personal victories on a pedestal rather than making them relatable to his audience. That's why I perceived his next step should be to focus on the audience.

That, in a nutshell, is the advice of this chapter. The more you focus on what you are doing for the benefit of your audience, the less you will focus on your own nerves, anxiety, or feelings of inadequacy. How do you focus on your audience? Start with knowing the purpose you have in serving them.

Yes, you read that correctly—*serving them*. How are you there to make a difference in your listeners' lives? To master your nerves and gain confidence in your speaking, you must start with a commitment to be of service, to make a difference to others. That commitment begins with knowing your specific purpose.

What are you there to accomplish?

If I were to ask you your purpose in speaking, you would most likely answer with two words, such as "to inform," "to educate," or perhaps "to persuade." If your purpose can be stated in two words, it is a *general* purpose. To truly know how you are going to serve your audience, you must know your *specific* purpose. Your specific purpose is the answer to this question: "What do I want my listeners to think, do, or feel differently when I am done?"

Every time you prepare a speech, you must keep this question in mind. Once you know the answer, it becomes the yardstick by which you measure every phrase, sentence, or paragraph: *Does this advance my specific purpose?* If you don't know what difference you are there to make in your listeners' lives, you are not yet ready to speak, no matter how polished you think you might be.

What difference do you want to make? Do you want to move your audience to action? If so, what is the one, specific action you want them to take? They are much more likely to act if you give them only one, specific next step. "Go to my website." "Find me on LinkedIn." "Sign up for my newsletter." These are all next steps I have heard speakers give their audiences (and have sometimes used myself).

What about *thinking* differently? This is harder to measure. How will you prompt your audience members to think differently about your topic? In a scientific presentation, for example, you might want your listeners to consider the difference your work has made in our state of knowledge about your field of research. In a business presentation, perhaps you will want to shift their attitude toward doing business with your company. However, in this case, it is likely that you also will want them to take action (e.g., do business with you). This illustrates the point that you often want your listeners to think, do, *and* feel differently when you are done. That is, look at ways to combine these verbs. Want someone to fund your research or your pet project? Chances are, you want them not only to write that check but also to *feel* that it is money well spent.

Put simply, you want to accomplish something when you speak. Knowing your specific purpose causes you to think about what you are accomplishing *for your audience*, and not simply for yourself, when you have the privilege of your audience's attention. The more audience-focused you are, the less likely you are to worry about how you come across.

What does your audience most need from you right now?

Another way to be audience-focused is to set aside all thoughts of what *you* need to accomplish by speaking (e.g., looking good and coming across as an expert) and to concentrate instead on your audience's needs. Why are they in that room at that particular time to hear you? (Or even in a virtual room as in the case of a webinar, for example.) What message from you will change their situation for the better? Or, looking beyond the message, what *experience* can they expect to receive from hearing you?

I know speakers who are all about the experience. It's what makes them memorable. That's not to say they don't have good messages as well. It's just that messages aren't always "sticky," to use a popular phrase. We're bombarded with so many messages daily, it's hard to make one message stick in a listener's mind. To make your message stick, you must connect with your audience in a memorable way. And that requires starting out with an understanding of what your audience needs from you.

An example will help make this clear. Some years back, I was put in charge of a training program to support the rollout of a new, digital radio technology used in television broadcasting. The people who would be using this technology were videographers and technicians at virtually all the TV stations in the United States that employ tools like news vans and helicopters to link live news and sporting events back to their newsrooms and studios. Those of us who were designing this training program were engineers, and we started from the assumption—which seemed reasonable to us engineers— that what these users of the new technology needed to be successful was information about how the technology worked. We felt a *need* to share with them what we knew about what lay "under the hood," so to speak, of the new technology.

Were we successful? In a word, no. We failed to make our message stick. Initial reviews of the training we delivered were lukewarm, at best.

Then I shifted my focus. I spent time with some users of the legacy technology that was about to be replaced. The people I spoke with represented the actual (not the imagined) target audience for our training. What they told me was eye-opening. They did not express curiosity about what lay under the hood. They expressed *fear* for what it would mean to them in doing their jobs. "I'm afraid I'll get yelled at." "I'm afraid of getting fired."

Our audience did not need most of the information we had compiled. What they needed was for someone to understand where they were emotionally.

Armed with this new understanding of our audience's needs, we redesigned a new training experience from the ground up. Our audience-driven purpose was to replace their fear with confidence that they could perform their job even better using the new technology. We showed them how this was the case for people who were already using it. We made our message stick because we gave them a training experience that addressed what *they* needed, not what we thought we needed to show them. We became audience-focused, not information-focused.

You can do this, too. Return to the questions at the beginning of this section. Why is your audience there? What is their situation? What experience can you give them that will change their situation for the better?

When you combine solid answers to those questions with a solid answer to the question of your specific purpose from earlier in the chapter, you will be well on your way to making a positive, memorable difference to your listeners.

How will you improve your listeners' condition?

Note that we are talking about making a *positive* difference to your listeners. You are not there to deliver information; you are there to improve something about your listeners' condition. How will they benefit from the *experience* of hearing you speak?

"How will I make my audience's lives better? Isn't that asking a lot of me?" you might wonder. Put that way, it does seem like a daunting task. But remember, they are giving you the gift of their attention. Isn't it only right that you give them something of value in return?

It is not egotistical to believe the experience of hearing you speak can improve someone else's condition. If you walk away believing that, you might get even more nervous about speaking than you already are! No, this point is about approaching an audience with the humility that comes from an attitude of *service*. When you perceive that you are there to provide a service to your listeners, and that by doing so you will help them grow in some way, then you are well on your way to being truly audience-focused.

Their growth can take many forms. Perhaps they will grow more confident that they can take control of some aspect of their lives—money, relationships, health, etc. Perhaps they will grow more knowledgeable about your topic. Perhaps they will gain a new skill. What will they get from you in return for the investment of their time and attention (and, perhaps, money)?

Here is an exercise. Get a sheet of paper or open to a blank page in your journal. Write down this question: "How will my audience benefit from hearing me talk?" When you are ready, close this book, set it aside, and write as many answers as you can to that question.

You're back! I hope you truly invested some time in that writing exercise. If so, do you now feel more confident to get in front of that audience and *serve* them? Remember, you are there not to impress but to serve. Approach a speaking opportunity with the heart of a servant. Focus on your audience's needs, not your own. This, I believe, was Rodrigo's missing ingredient. He had the requisite skills. If he lacked anything, it was (perhaps) a bit of humility.

Nervousness when speaking might be a sign you are not prepared. (In that case, stay tuned for Chapter 3.) Or, it might be a sign that you are too focused on how you are going to appear to your audience. A focus on the audience's needs and how you are going to meet them—with a sense of purpose and an attitude of service—will go a long way toward easing your anxiety. Focus on your audience, and not on yourself.

CHAPTER 3

Your key to success: the right kind of preparation

"Before anything else, preparation is the key to success."

—ALEXANDER GRAHAM BELL

As stated in <u>Chapter 2</u>, nervousness when speaking can arise from a feeling that you are being called upon to do something for which you are not adequately prepared. But what does "adequately prepared" mean? Does it mean having your lines memorized like an actor in a play? Does it mean having your speech written out so you can read it word for word, and thereby have the confidence that you are going to say exactly what you planned to say? Does it mean being so familiar with your material that you can just get up and "wing it"? Or is preparation something else altogether? In this chapter, you will pick up some tips and ideas that will help you feel more prepared in the most common speaking situations you are likely to encounter.

Write your speech but don't read it

In most speaking situations, you don't want to read a speech. Exceptions include (but are not limited to) these:

- Political speeches
- Management speeches in which you are delivering critical information
- Eulogies and other formal occasions

On such occasions as these, it's important to stick to the script. Going off-script in the moment can have undesirable results.

However, it's important to realize that being too dependent on your script can also lead to undesired results. Picture (or recall, if you can) a speaker whose attention is focused on his or her script. What do you see? Unless the speaker is using a Teleprompter®, you are probably seeing far too much of the top of that speaker's head as he or she looks down at the script. And unless the speaker is particularly skilled at delivering a speech in this way, you probably are not seeing a strong connection between the speaker and the audience. Reading a script puts a barrier between speaker and audience. That's not to say it's impossible to overcome that barrier, but it does make your job harder.

It's easier to forge a strong connection with your audience when you can make more eye contact and be more conversational in your delivery. Both of these attributes are easier to achieve when you are less dependent on your script. So let's look at how to get there while still being better prepared than someone who is "winging it."

I strongly advocate writing out what you plan to say as part of your preparation process. Here are four reasons:

1. Writing your speech sharpens your thinking about what you plan to say.
2. Writing your speech gives you the opportunity for better wordsmithing.
3. "Great speeches aren't written—they're *re*written." (I don't know who originated that.) You cannot edit, and therefore improve, what has not yet been created and written down.
4. As a practical matter, writing your speech—at least if you write in a word-processing program like Microsoft Word— gives you a word count, which tells you how long your speech is going to take. Most people speak at a rate of 125 to 150 words per minute. So if you're scheduled to give a ten-minute speech, you'd better not have more than 1,250 to 1,500 words. If you have 2,000, then you still have some work to do.

But one factor works *against* writing out your speech, and you might have already thought of it. When someone writes a speech and then reads it, it often sounds stilted or unnatural. That's because it takes time and practice to learn to write in your "speaking voice." Most beginning speakers—and many experienced ones—lack this skill.

Fortunately, there is an easy work-around for this problem. But before I tell you what it is, let's consider what I mean by your speaking voice compared with your writing voice. The two differ in intent, in word choice, and in structure or syntax.

The written word has a certain permanence to it. The reader can reread what is written, evaluate it, and draw additional meaning from it that might have been overlooked the first time. The listener has no such ability when hearing the spoken word. Furthermore, the writer does not encounter the reader in the way the speaker encounters the listener. When I speak to you, I can tell by your feedback—both spoken and unspoken—how well I have conveyed an idea. The writer has no channel for such immediate feedback. That is why the writer's intent must be to make things absolutely as clear as possible to any reader who later encounters that text, and to do so while honoring the mechanics of grammar, word choice, spelling, punctuation, and tone (i.e., level of formality).

The speaker's intent, on the other hand, is to make a connection with the listener in the moment, and to be as clear as possible moment by moment because the listener does not have the luxury of re-hearing what has been said. Because the intent is different, the tools and mechanics are different as well. When you speak, you tend to use a more limited vocabulary than when you write—and that is a good thing, because your listener cannot pause you to look up a word. To retain the connection with your listener, you must also use simpler sentence structure. In written English, a writer has the choice of making complex, convoluted sentences using multiple subordinate clauses. He does so knowing that the reader can, if necessary, go back and re-read such a sentence if the meaning is not clear the first time. Because that is not a choice available to the listener, the speaker must choose to keep sentence structure simpler.

In short, when you are speaking you need to simplify your vocabulary and sentence structure. And your listeners will tend to be more forgiving of grammatical shortcuts since they do not linger on the page.

So what is this promised work-around? It is to *use* your speaking voice until you are sufficiently practiced at *writing* in your speaking voice. The technique is simple. You will need a table and two chairs, two cups of coffee or tea, a recording device, and a friend. Sit down over your favorite beverage and casually *talk through* what you have to say with a friend. You can certainly use an outline or notes. Be sure to record everything. I use a dedicated, digital voice recorder that is readily available at electronics or office-supply stores, but you can use an app on your phone just as easily.

The key requirement for your listener is to be someone whose level of education and background knowledge of your topic is similar to that of your intended audience. If your friend knows too much already about your topic, you are likely to skip over background information that might prove essential to your audience's understanding.

When you have finished talking through your outline or notes, stop the recorder and find someone to transcribe the conversation for you. Even if you are skilled at transcription, I recommend using someone else—it is not hard to find such services online—because then you won't be tempted to edit as you transcribe.

Once you have the transcription, edit it for structure, clarity, and—if necessary—time, using the formula of 125 to 150 words per minute of allotted speaking time. Congratulations! Now you have a first draft of your speech, which is likely to be more conversational than it would have been otherwise. This will help you connect with your audience and sound well-prepared.

Internalize a lot, memorize a little

As stated at the top of the chapter, you want to write a speech but in most cases don't want to *read* a speech. What do you do instead? You *internalize* it. This means you become intimately familiar with what you have written so that your listeners can benefit from the careful wordsmithing you have done while still getting the feeling that you are *talking* to them and not reading to them.

You are trying to come across as well-prepared and yet in the moment. Sounds impossible, right? It's not, if you use the right kind of preparation. Here are the basic steps:

1. Memorize your opening 30 seconds.
2. Memorize key transitions throughout the speech.
3. Memorize your closing 30 seconds.

Once you have committed those passages to memory, you simply need to know the rest of the material well enough to deliver it extemporaneously. Your careful wordsmithing will show up in the open, the close, and the key transitions between points. Why the transitions? Because they keep your mental road map of the speech front and center in your mind. Think about memorizing the directions to get to a friend's house. What do you commit to memory? The turns! What happens between those turns might be fascinating, but it is the turns that you need to get right or you'll go off course. The same is true of your speech. Know where and how you are turning as you move from one story or point to the next.

Do you struggle with memorization? Many speakers do, and that struggle adds to their anxiety about speaking. Here is a technique that works well for me: learn your speech back to front. This is just the opposite of what seems to be the natural way to do it, and it works! Most people start at the beginning of a speech, practicing that over and over and adding a bit more each time. The problem with that approach is you become less confident in your internalization as you go. Hence, you are more likely to stumble, which will make you even more self-conscious.

Instead, work backward from the end. Start by repeating the last sentence of your speech until it is committed to memory. Then add the sentence before it. Continue in this way until you can deliver the last 30 seconds (or so) of your speech fluently, without having to stop and think about it.

Now look at your manuscript. Highlight the key transitions and any places where you feel your exact wording is critical. Continue working backward, internalizing the speech one chunk of content at a time, with careful attention to the highlighted lines. Elsewhere, you can allow yourself to deviate from the exact wording. You might even find a smoother, more streamlined and conversational way to say something than what you originally wrote down. Congratulations—you are being extemporaneous! And as long as you do so with careful attention to the highlighted lines, you still have the benefit of your structure and wordsmithing.

Finally, memorize the opening 30 seconds as you did the close. Now you are done. Continue rehearsing until you are confident of your ability to get all the way through the speech without having to strain to remember what comes next.

Here is another technique that can help with internalizing your speech: add movement to your rehearsal. Obviously, this will not work for a speech that has to be delivered from behind a lectern. But for any speech where you are free to use the stage or other speaking area, you want to plan how you are going to move as you deliver your speech. Perhaps you want to place your three main points at distinct locations on the stage. Is your speech arranged chronologically? Think of presenting it on a visual timeline, proceeding from your audience's left to right. Once you have planned how you are going to move through your speech, introduce that movement while you are still internalizing. You are likely to find that knowing where you are and how you are moving at a certain point—say, a transition line—will help you recall that line more clearly. It's a form of visualization, but it goes beyond the visual to include the kinesthetic. Try it! I think you'll be surprised at how well it works.

Prepare for a strong ending

You have prepared your speech. You have crafted and honed your best stories. You have memorized those stories and your transitions and internalized the rest while you practiced your intentional movements across the stage. You're ready, right? Well, there is one more thing you might want to do. Depending on the nature of your talk, you may be expected to take questions from your audience. By its very nature, a question-and-answer (Q&A) session is unscripted. But that does not mean you can't prepare for it.

The first thing to know about preparing for a Q&A session is that it should never be the last content your audience hears from you. Read that sentence again. *It should never be the last thing they hear!* That likely goes against everything you have seen done by other speakers. But think about it: What are audiences most likely to remember? The first impression you make, the most startling or novel claim you make, and the last words they hear you say. If you want to be remembered as a well-prepared, confident speaker, then those last words should never be, "Well…if there are no more questions, then…thank you very much." How memorable is that?

Instead, here is what you do. You save concluding remarks for *after* the Q&A. This might be a story or some other way of summing up your talk and leaving your listeners something to "chew on," so to speak. Your concluding remarks should take no more than about two minutes. As you approach the end of your allotted speaking time, you cue your audience as to what is to come by saying, "Before I give you my concluding remarks, I have a few minutes to take your questions. Who has the first one to get us started?" Then, at the two-minute mark, you say, "That's all the questions we have time for now. As promised, here are my concluding remarks…" and then you move smoothly into your well-prepared closing.

As for handling the questions themselves, you can prepare for this element by using a friendly test audience. Your speech need not even be in its final form. Talk through your content (perhaps this is when you want to record it for transcription as a first draft) with someone who has a similar level of background knowledge as your intended audience and see what questions linger in their minds. You may choose to address them explicitly within your revised speech, or you may simply want to be prepared when someone in your final audience asks the same question. Either way, you want to practice appearing at ease with questions. One way to do this is to be sure to repeat each question before you answer it. This accomplishes several purposes. It ensures an accurate understanding of the question, it honors the person who has asked it, it ensures everyone in the audience hears it, and it gives you a few seconds to pause for breath (and thought) before answering. All of which will help you feel and appear more confident and in control of the situation.

Practice in front of Toastmasters

The subject of preparation would not be complete without a plug for Toastmasters International, the organization dedicated to helping its members develop communication and leadership skills. Need a test audience? A Toastmasters club is a safe environment where you can expect to get useful feedback. If you are not already familiar with Toastmasters, go to the website, click on "Find a Club," and enter your location. Chances are good that you will find multiple clubs near you, meeting at different times of day. Choose the most convenient one and go—it costs nothing to visit. And if you decide to join, dues are quite reasonable.

What can you expect to get from attending Toastmasters? A supportive group of like-minded individuals who are practiced (as you will become) at listening to presentations and giving feedback on them. You will be able to choose an educational path that is tailored to your own speaking goals, and as you proceed along that path you will gain confidence as you pick up and practice new skills. Depending on the practices of your particular club, you may even be able to rehearse an entire keynote or other long presentation in front of your supportive club audience.

One thing to keep in mind about Toastmasters is that it is a long-term time investment. In most clubs, you may have the opportunity to present a speech only every couple of months or so, depending on the number of members and the length of the meetings. An alternative that may give you faster results is to find out if a club in your area is offering a Speechcraft program. These six- to eight-week programs, offered from time to time by experienced Toastmasters, are aimed at presenting the fundamentals of public speaking to non-members. Generally, Speechcraft participants are given weekly speaking assignments—so if one is available to you, it could be a way to make progress more quickly in the short term.

When it comes to presenting with confidence, preparation is the key. In this chapter, you have picked up tips for preparing your material, learning your material, and practicing your material. If you put these tools to use, you will find your anxiety level trending downward as your confidence grows. However, you may still feel nervous and wonder how to deal with those feelings. The next chapter will give you eight practical tips you can incorporate into your very next presentation—whether in Toastmasters or elsewhere—to overcome those nervous feelings.

CHAPTER 4

Fight nervousness with these simple tips

"Our anxiety does not come from thinking about the future, but from wanting to control it."

—KAHLIL GIBRAN

You know your message has power and that you deserve to deliver it. You have done the work of focusing on your audience and what you are there to do for them. You have fully prepared for the task of delivering your message. And still, when the time comes, you are nervous. You feel the adrenaline rising as your palms sweat, your heart races, and your breathing becomes shallow. Maybe your stomach is churning. Those are physical manifestations of your mind's fight-or-flight response. What can you do to overcome those sensations? Can they even be overcome? The answer is, they can be managed. This chapter contains eight practical tips you can use to calm your body and mind so you can be fully present with your audience and accomplish your purpose in speaking to them.

Tip #1: Keep in mind the 10-to-1 rule

I learned this "rule" from the 1999 World Champion of Public Speaking, Craig Valentine. It goes something like this: *No matter how nervous you may feel or how much you think your nerves are showing, your nervousness looms ten times larger in your own mind than anything the audience will perceive.* You think your palms are sweating? If you don't wipe them on your pants, the audience will never know. Knees shaking? Completely invisible from the second row. Voice quavering? The audience might notice that a little—but a pause for a deep breath will command their attention even more.

In other words, the audience is not perceiving more than a fraction of the anxiety you are feeling, so why broadcast your nervousness to the world?

Tip #2: Use your nervous energy to your advantage

I have spent thousands of hours in front of tens of thousands of audience members. I have competed twice in the penultimate stage of the World Championship of Public Speaking. But if you think I don't get nervous before I walk out in front of an audience, you're mistaken!

Nervousness is a defense mechanism. It simply reflects a heightened state of arousal to the possibility of a threat. Am I facing a threat when I walk out on stage to speak? Only in the sense that I might let my audience down and think less of myself for it. So I use my awareness of that possible outcome to steel myself against it. I use my nerves to ensure I am serving my audience well.

How do I do that? By channeling that energy where it will do the most good. And that starts by being aware of my mental and physical state so I can choose how to alter it. When you feel threatened, your body tends to respond by pouring adrenaline into your bloodstream. This is a wonderful defense mechanism when you are facing an external, physical threat. Under the influence of adrenaline, you can run faster, hit harder, and jump higher than you could without it. You can get yourself out of a close encounter with a saber-toothed tiger.

The downside of an adrenaline rush, though, is that blood flow is diverted to your large muscles and your mental energy is narrowed to the immediate threat that is right in front of you. Is that saber-toothed tiger a threat? Quite likely. But is that audience a threat?

In a word, no. Your audience *wants* you to succeed. They want to hear a good speech. They are pulling for you. The threat is not the audience. The threat is your fear of embarrassing yourself in front of an audience.

But that fear is rooted in your self-consciousness. It is all about the question, "Am I going to look good?" When you practice replacing that with the question, "How am I going to use my energy to serve this audience's needs?" then you begin to move away from feeling that the spotlight is on you to succeed or fail. Instead, you mentally turn that spotlight around and shine it on your audience. Focus your energy on what your audience needs and how you are there to serve that need. In general terms, they probably need information from a trusted source. Or they may need reassurance, inspiration, or a call to action. Whatever they need, focus on giving it to them. What they do *not* need is a speaker who is too worried about appearing in control to be fully present.

Tip #3: Use positive affirmations

Once you have convinced yourself that your goal is serving your audience instead of looking good, the logical next step is to affirm, verbally, your intent and ability to do so. Many speakers find that using positive affirmations is an effective tool for taking their minds off their nerves so they can be present with their audience. Here are some examples of positive, affirming statements you can make to yourself right before you go onstage:

"I am uniquely qualified to deliver *this* message to *this* audience."

"I am fully present with my audience."

"These people are eager to hear me, like me, and learn from me."

"This audience *wants* me to succeed."

"I know I will do a good job because I am here to serve."

You can probably think of other affirming statements you can make to yourself. Let them help you to be centered on serving your audience so you can be fully present in the task of doing so.

Tip #4: Tap into postural feedback

What exactly is postural feedback? In short, it is the new name for what was called "power poses" starting about eight years ago, before the research behind it became embroiled in scientific controversy. Harvard researcher Amy Cuddy, in a widely viewed 2012 TED talk[1], described her research showing that merely adopting a powerful body position (think Rocky at the top of those steps) can have an impact on how we think and feel about ourselves. She also reported finding measurable changes in stress hormone levels when test subjects adopted such poses. (These latter findings were disputed by other researchers. For a nicely nuanced response, read the article cited below[2].)

In short, if you carry yourself like a powerful, confident person, the body-mind feedback loop will start to convince you that you *are* more powerful and confident. Therefore, before you go onstage or walk into the meeting room, adopt a powerful pose for a couple of minutes. Stand like a champion fighter with your arms outstretched and above shoulder level. Or, if you prefer, stand like Wonder Woman: chin up, fists on hips.

If you want to use some positive affirmations at the same time, so much the better. Start by declaring that you are powerful and confident, and you will carry the audience along with you.

Tip #5: Meditate

For many people—myself included—meditation is a way of achieving and reinforcing mindfulness, or the practice of being present in the moment, whatever that moment may bring. I believe this can be quite helpful to anyone who struggles with nervousness when speaking. If, just before you go on stage or to the front of the room, you are able to center yourself in the moment, you are likely to find your breathing and heart rate slowing and your attention shifting away from "looking good" in the front of your audience and more toward *serving* that audience in some beneficial way.

How do you meditate? Developing a meditation practice is beyond the scope of this chapter. There are many excellent resources available to help you. One that I have used is called *The Mindful Way Workbook* by John Teasdale, et al.

When I meditate, I often choose to fix my mind on a positive message. I suppose you could say I am mixing meditation with positive affirmations, mentioned above. I choose to do this because I have often found my "inner critic" to be my biggest stumbling block to success. That's the little voice inside me (described in Chapter 1) that tries to convince me that my message is useless, my speaking skills are lacking, and no one truly wants to hear (or read) what I have to say. To counter that pattern of negative thinking—for that is what it is—I often meditate on words I learned from author and speaker Brené Brown, which I found in her book *Daring Greatly*. Those words are simply: "I am enough."[3]

The important thing to me about using this phrase is not to let qualifiers sneak in. It can't be, "I *would* be enough if…" or "I *will* be enough when…" Also, it is not about being enough *of* anything. Not "I am smart enough"…"I am capable enough"…"I am articulate enough." No, it is simply a reflection of the fact that *in this moment*, in this endeavor, in this wanting to share myself and my message for the benefit of others, *I* am enough. I am enough to make a difference. What I might have done before, what I might yet do in the future—these are irrelevant. I am in the present, and I am enough.

Of course, there is a difference between saying these words to yourself and truly believing them. That is why, for me, meditating on this phrase is an ongoing process. I believe those words more now than I did years ago when I started saying them. And I trust that I will believe them even more in the future. What I do know is that these words have helped me break free of self-imposed limitations. Want proof? It is in your hands. This is the third book I have written since I began the process of confronting my inner critic by meditating on my enough-ness.

What could you accomplish, and what audiences could you influence, if you truly believed that you are enough?

Tip #6: Hydrate

The last three tips in this chapter address your physical preparation for the taxing task of speaking in front of an audience. The first is: hydrate. And stay hydrated. Do not approach the lectern without first drinking an adequate amount of water or other non-caffeinated, non-alcoholic beverage; and, second, ensuring that, for any speech longer than about five minutes, water is available at the lectern.

Fewer things will elevate your distress in front of an audience more quickly than a sudden attack of dry mouth or a tight throat. Both are signs of tension that will be exacerbated by inadequate hydration. You want to keep your vocal mechanism moist and well lubricated, so drink plenty of water.

And here's a pro tip: When you pause for a drink while speaking, drink from a glass rather than a bottle. Here's why: drinking from a bottle generally requires you to tip your head back further than sipping from a glass. While it may seem like a trivial difference, the effect of this is to break your connection with the audience. Don't believe me? Watch another speaker or check yourself on video. Drinking from a glass is simply smoother and less distracting to the audience.

Tip #7: Rest

Besides being well hydrated, the other best practice for physical preparation is to be well rested before you speak. While this may seem obvious, there are factors that often work against the speaker when it comes to sufficient rest.

Let's look at some of those factors:

• **Travel**—As a frequent speaker and seminar presenter, I have traveled extensively. I know just how travel can disrupt one's systems, especially sleep patterns. I have spent years in "road warrior" mode: giving a seminar one day, traveling to the next city afterward, and repeating the process the next day. This is not good for one's sleep! I admit I grew somewhat accustomed to it over time. However, when it comes time to travel to a conference or other event for a major speaking engagement, I always make sure I give myself enough buffer time between travel and speaking. Besides, arriving at a conference the day before I speak gives me a great opportunity to mill around with other attendees, getting an idea what they are experiencing and what their concerns are. When you must travel to speak, always give careful thought to your travel times and leave time for unforeseen delays.

- **Late preparation**—I will freely admit to some late-night sessions spent finalizing the material for a presentation. But I do not recommend it. So many things are beyond your control; don't let your preparation timeline be one of them. Have a presentation coming up in two months? Now is not too early to start preparing. Work backward, not from your presentation date but from the date of your *final rehearsal*, and figure out when you need to have your visuals ready (the last step), when you need to have the whole presentation *written* (yes, I do recommend writing it—but not reading it), and therefore when you need to start collecting your information and outlining or mind-mapping or whatever you do to get started. Don't put it off! A lot of preparation goes into giving a good presentation. Don't cheat yourself and your audience by trying to do it all at the last minute.
- **Stress**—For most of us, getting in front of an audience involves a certain amount of stress. I've been doing it for years, in front of a total audience that numbers well into the thousands, and I still feel it. When I no longer feel *any* stress about getting in front of an audience, I think that will be the time to stop doing it, because it will probably mean I

have given up caring about my audience's experience.
When you care about your audience—as you should—you
will naturally feel somewhat stressed about whether they are
getting what they need from you. This is to be expected;
and, as described in Tip #2, it leads to a nervousness that
you can use to your advantage. Meanwhile, don't lose sleep
over it. When I occasionally struggle to go to sleep because
of something looming over me the next day, I ask myself
this question: "What is the best thing I can be doing right
now to be ready for tomorrow?" And invariably, the answer
is, "Get some sleep." Then I roll over and go to sleep. Try
it!

You owe it to your audience to be at your best physically and mentally when you are expecting them to give you their attention. Therefore, make it a point to be well rested by the time you arrive on that stage, because that will affect you both physically and mentally.

Tip #8: Breathe

Remember, any physiological signs of stress will loom ten times larger in your own mind than anything your audience will perceive. So how do you tamp down those feelings of nervousness so they don't overwhelm you? The final tip is simply this: *breathe*. When you've done everything else to prepare yourself mentally and physically for the challenge of putting yourself out there in front of an audience, don't forget to simply take a few deep, calming breaths. This will help you slow your pounding heart and even reduce the concentration of the stress hormone cortisol in your bloodstream.

I am not going to offer you a one-size-fits-all formula of how many breaths to take over how many counts; I'm going to trust you to find what works for you. Here is what has worked for me, and you can draw on my experience if it helps you. Decades ago, as an undergraduate, I took a couple of years of voice lessons. The most powerful thing Dr. Amaya taught me was how to breathe as a singer, by fully opening my throat and quickly expanding around my diaphragm. Doing this well takes practice to coordinate the timely interaction of the different muscles involved. But it was worth learning, for two primary reasons: It makes my breathing virtually inaudible because it forces my throat open, and it gives me the confidence of knowing that I can quickly catch my breath when necessary without interrupting the rhythm of my speech.

If you have ever felt desperately out of breath while speaking, then you know what happens when you are not breathing well. Chances are, your throat is tightening up as you try to conserve whatever breath you have left, and you are not taking the time to fully re-inflate your lungs. So try practicing slowly at first. Concentrate on fully opening your throat by dropping your larynx (men, that's your Adam's apple), and then try to develop the sensation of filling your lungs from the bottom up. Practice it to get the timing down: larynx goes down, belly goes out. When you can do it quickly, you will never need to worry about running out of breath. And even when you do it slowly, you should feel the calming effect that comes of being well-oxygenated.

By the way, when you hear a radio or a television announcer, or an audiobook narrator, who takes audible, almost gasping breaths, you will know that this is a person who has not been trained in proper breathing technique. You can do better!

The bottom line is this: You need to take some slow, calming breaths before you speak, and you need to know how to breathe effectively while you are speaking. Practice until you find what works for you in both situations, and you will gain a sense of confidence and control under stress.

There you have it: eight practical tips you can employ right away to help you overcome nerves and tension when you speak. These tips will help you in all kinds of speaking situations, and in front of almost any audience. Still, some audiences are more intimidating than others. The special case of presenting to high-level decision-makers is covered in the next chapter.

---

[1] https://www.ted.com/talks/amy_cuddy_your_body_language_may_shape_who_you_are

[2] https://ideas.ted.com/inside-the-debate-about-power-posing-a-q-a-with-amy-cuddy/

[3] Brené Brown, *Daring Greatly: How the Courage to be Vulnerable Transforms the Way We Live, Love, Parent, and Lead* (New York: Gotham Books, 2012)

CHAPTER 5

Don't bore the board: presenting to a high-status audience

"High achievement always takes place in the framework of high expectation."

—CHARLES F. KETTERING

Few occasions are more likely to bring on a case of dry mouth and wobbly knees than having to present to a high-status audience like a Board of Directors or a gathering of C-suite executives. How does one overcome the nervousness that goes with such appearances? Does one even *want* to overcome nervousness in those situations?

I would say you do want to bring your nerves under control, even if—as described in Chapter 4—you have learned to use your nervous energy to your advantage. I say this because you want your message to be well-received, and that requires that you make a favorable first impression. Harvard researcher Amy Cuddy (mentioned in the previous chapter) says in her book *Presence*[1] that we form first impressions very quickly by answering two questions subconsciously:

1. Can I trust this person?
2. Is this person capable of doing something useful for me?

In psychological terms, we are assessing *warmth* and *competence*. What I find interesting is that we assess these two dimensions in a specific order: warmth first, then competence.

Consider how this plays out If you are trying to influence a high-ranking group of decision-makers. Before they weigh the value of your evidence (*competence*), they must first decide if you are a trustworthy source of information (*warmth*). If, when you introduce yourself, your palms are sweaty, your breathing is rapid and shallow, or your gaze is averted—any of which could happen if your nerves are getting the better of you—then you may "read" as someone who has something to hide. This is clearly not the impression you want to make.

Given that you want to come across as capable, trustworthy, and in control of the situation, it is important to overcome excessive nervousness. If you have read and put into practice the preceding four chapters, you should be well on your way to doing so. Still, there are three specific tips you might want to keep in mind in this high-stress situation.

Tip #1: Don't rely on your visual aids

In any speaking situation, I always advise my clients, "Be ready to give any presentation without slides, because sooner or later technology will fail you." This is doubly true when you are presenting to high-level decision-makers. Their time is valuable to the organization they serve; they are expected to make the most of it. Not only will they be impatient with any sign of technological difficulty, but also boardrooms often are not set up with good sightlines to a screen or monitor.

Besides that, there is a tendency to assume—rightly or wrongly—that much of what is contained in slides is designed to obfuscate, not to clarify. Therefore, don't be surprised if you go into a board meeting and you're told, "Skip the slides; just tell us what we need to know and why."

If you do need to share visuals with such an audience, therefore, be doubly well-prepared. To start with, be sure you have applied your specific purpose (see Chapter 2) as a filter to strain out any unnecessary visual content. Show only what is truly necessary to support your case for the recommended course of action. Second, if it is essential that the decision-makers have such information in front of them at decision-making time, consider putting it into a handout.

Above all, do not allow yourself to be dependent on your slideware to get you through the presentation. You should not have to be able to see either your bullet points on the slides or the accompanying speaker notes in order to deliver your presentation. (Remember, *you* are the presentation; your slides are merely the *visual aid*.)

If you have crafted a well-structured talk, you should not have any trouble remembering it. If there are specific details that need to be cited accurately, read them from a note card. This demonstrates your commitment to getting the details right.

Tip #2: Get to the point quickly with a specific narrative tool

When you present to high-level decision-makers, they expect you to demonstrate your competence and tell them what they need to know. But, as we have seen, they will be subconsciously assessing your warmth (trustworthiness) before anything else. Therefore, you need a plan for accomplishing both objectives quickly.

The solution to this challenge is to use a specific storytelling structure that I have not introduced previously. It's a structure I have just demonstrated to you. Look again at the preceding paragraph, paying particular attention to the conjunctions. What are they? *"And…but…therefore."* (Strictly speaking, "therefore" is a conjunctive adverb—close enough!)

This "and/but/therefore" (or ABT) construction has been identified by scientist-turned-filmmaker Randy Olson, Ph.D., as the key to understanding narrative structure.[2] Think of it like a very short, three-act play. We have an initial condition: Your audience expects you to demonstrate your competence and tell them what they need to know. That's Act One.

Then, there's a contradiction introduced by the word *but*: "But…they will be subconsciously assessing your warmth (trustworthiness) before anything else." In literary terms, this is described as the "inciting incident." It's really where the story begins. At this point, as Dr. Olson says, we've entered the narrative world and different parts of the brain have become active.

We want to know the answer to the question or the relief of the tension that is set up in Act Two, so we turn to *therefore*, a consequence word. "Therefore, you need a plan for accomplishing both objectives quickly." This brings us to Act Three.

It sounds simple and formulaic. And it works.

Consider the difference between these two openings:

Opening 1: "Thank you for letting me be here today to tell you about our new marketing initiative. As you can see from this slide, our market share in rechargeable widgets has not kept pace with our goals. And our marketing budget has shrunk as a percent of overhead. Our competitors are starting to overtake our position, and leading indicators are showing an unhealthy trend. We believe it is only a matter of time before this puts pressure on our bottom line."

Opening 2: "For the past five years, our company has held the dominant market position in rechargeable widgets, and the strategic vision document this board approved calls for committing the resources to maintain that dominance. But our competitors' aggressive marketing to key demographics is starting to hurt our market share. Therefore, we believe ABC Company needs to back up its commitment with a strategic infusion of marketing resources in the following three areas…"

Which option sounds more persuasive to you? The one that takes five sentences and still has not laid out an action plan, or the one that leads into specific recommendations in the third sentence? That is the kind of focused communication top-level decision-makers will appreciate. Also, because the speaker starts with what is already known, he or she comes across as trustworthy and believable. The listeners will get caught up in the narrative about the competitors' threat and the action they can take to counter it. As the numbers unfold later, the speaker will have created a context for understanding them. In fact, the speaker can return to the ABT structure more than once, guiding the listeners through the unfolding story toward the conclusion.

You need to get to the point quickly, and you need to come across as a trusted expert. But that's hard to do in a few sentences without a plan. Therefore, you need the ABT structure!

Tip #3: Practice, practice, practice!

Who is this high-status audience, anyway? Are they going to decide whether to do business with your company? Are they going to approve your strategic initiative? Are they going to see you as executive material?

Whoever they are, you may have a lot riding on this presentation. That's probably why you are nervous about it.

What is surprising to me, as a speaking coach, is how many people in such a situation will simply throw together an outline and a slideware file, put on a tie, think through their presentation once, and call themselves prepared. What are they leaving out? *Practice!*

When you have a lot riding on a presentation, there is no excuse for not rehearsing it. You are there to impress your audience with your thoughtful analysis, your insight, and your efficiency in using their time to make your point. Those elements do not just happen. Like any project, they depend on careful planning and execution. You have prepared your content; now you must prepare to deliver it in a convincing fashion. And that takes practice.

Are you using visual aids? If so, you must practice until you can move between images smoothly and without looking at the screen. Then, as stated previously, you must practice until you can give the presentation *without* visual aids. This is important, because too many presenters become dependent on their visuals. When forced to present without them—as will happen at some point—they become flustered and disoriented.

Everyone has access to video nowadays, so use that to your advantage. Record yourself rehearsing your presentation, in front of a test audience if possible. (What? You don't have a safe audience to practice on? Join Toastmasters!) Once you have recorded yourself, don't just watch it. View your recording strategically, by using these four steps:

Step 1: Watch the video with the sound turned off. That's right—don't listen to it! On this first pass, start to develop the habit of asking questions about the *speaker* in third person. This will help you begin to be more objective than we can typically be when watching ourselves on video. (Not hearing your own voice will help with this.) Don't ask "What do *I* look like?" or "What the heck was *I* doing?" Instead, ask questions like, "How well does the speaker use the stage? What is the speaker's body language saying here? How well does the speaker seem to be engaged with the audience? Where is that engagement the strongest or the weakest?"

Step 2: Turn your back to the screen (or turn your video monitor off) and just listen. This is the opposite of Step 1. Now you want sound and no visual. Again, ask your questions in the third person: Does the speaker have a coherent message? Does she deliver it without repeating herself or stumbling over transitions? Are the stories engaging and clearly related to his points? Is his intention clear? Do I understand what the speaker

wants the listeners to think, do, or feel
differently by the end?

Step 3: Watch the video again, but at faster-than-normal
playback speed. This is not hard to do with most video
programs. Chances are, you won't have audio, and
that's fine. This time you are watching for repeated
physical mannerisms that will become evident when
you speed up the video. What does the speaker do with
his hands? Does she push her hair back frequently? If
you think you're watching a tennis match, perhaps the
speaker paces back and forth excessively. These are
the kinds of things that come out when you watch it
sped up.

Step 4: Watch and listen normally. Be sure to save this step
for last. Now that you have practiced some third-
person objectivity in your viewing, apply that here.
How well does the speaker hold your attention? How
would you rate the speaker's overall effectiveness?
Are the voice, body, and face congruent with the
words being spoken? Does the speaker come across as
someone relatable? What would you advise the
speaker to do differently next time?

Watching yourself on video is bound to make you uncomfortable at first;
this is normal. That is no excuse for not doing it. Even if you don't have a test
audience, it is imperative that you rehearse repeatedly until you are well
prepared. Video is a tool for making the most of those rehearsals. There is not
much point in rehearsing something over and over again if you are doing it
badly each time. That is simply a recipe for getting worse, faster! Instead, use
feedback from others (e.g., a Toastmasters club) or from the objective eye of
the camera to identify areas for improvement, and then incorporate those
improvements into subsequent rehearsals.

Whatever you do, do *not* go into a high-stakes presentation unprepared. In
times of stress, you will fall back on what you have rehearsed. Have you
rehearsed giving an effective, persuasive presentation? Or merely rehearsed
looking at your slides or speaker notes? The difference will be obvious to

anyone in your audience.

<hr>

[1] Amy Cuddy, *Presence: Bringing Your Boldest Self to Your Biggest Challenges* (New York: Little, Brown and Company, 2013)

[2] Randy Olson, *Houston, We Have a Narrative: Why Science Needs Story* (Chicago: The University of Chicago Press, 2015)

CHAPTER 6

Handle emotional content like the pros

"Your intellect may be confused, but your emotions will never lie to you."

—ROGER EBERT

In your speaking career, there may come a time when you are required to deliver a message that carries emotional weight for you. Perhaps it is a toast at your child's wedding. Or accepting the congratulations of your peers at your retirement party. Or perhaps it will be a eulogy for a loved one. You may be overjoyed, or you may be grieving; either way, it can be hard to maintain your composure in such circumstances. Short of shutting yourself off emotionally—and thereby depriving your audience of a level of authenticity in your delivery—how do you manage your own emotions when the words you need to say get stuck in your throat and the tears start to well up?

Here, I must inject a personal note. My wife is an ordained pastor serving in the United Methodist Church. Some of the content of this chapter is based on my observations of her experiences in the church and is used with her permission.

For example, early in my wife's ministry she had to officiate at the funeral of a one-week-old infant. The family members were, of course, devastated by this loss—as was my wife. She came to me and said, "With all your speaking experience and stage training, what can you tell me that will help me make it through this funeral homily without breaking down in tears?" After giving her a hug, I offered the following advice: Practice until you can say it without choking up.

Repetition helps take the edge off

When you have words to say that cause your throat to tighten as you choke back emotion, the best place to start is with the same advice from Chapter 5: practice, practice, practice. After a while, those words will lose their power to choke you up as they become more familiar. They will become "just words" and not a fresh thought. Yes, this means that to some extent you are hardening yourself against their emotional power. So how do you walk the fine line between losing composure and losing the authenticity of that emotional moment?

The flip side of practicing until you numb (somewhat) the emotional weight of the message is to use the actor's trick known as *emotional substitution*.

To illustrate this, I turn to an experience of my own as an actor.

In 2008, I auditioned for a role in a play titled *Jacob Marley's Christmas Carol* by Tom Mula. One of the scenes I was given to read was very emotional. A character was recalling his experience, as a small child, of watching his mother die. The first time I read that scene in the audition, it was so powerfully written that I genuinely teared up as I inhabited that character's memory. Whether owing to those tears or not, I got the part.

Now the challenge became keeping that moment as fresh for each night's audience as it was for me the first time I read it. The repetition of those lines, in rehearsal after rehearsal and in performance after performance, dulled their impact on me. The tears, predictably, stopped coming.

The solution was emotional substitution. At the time of that play, I was more than a decade past my own father's unexpected death. Yet, recalling that time—which was not hard, as it was around the same time of year—still carried an emotional impact for me. I could substitute a feeling that was impactful yet manageable given the separation in time. Between that and the power of the playwright's words, I feel confident that each audience experienced the freshness of what the characters were experiencing on stage. Even though that freshness—like everything else on the stage—was an illusion created by the performers.

Many speakers are skeptical of using acting techniques on the platform (or in the pulpit). To that, I say speaking always involves acting. A mentor of mine, Kevin Burke, is an actor who gave more than 4,000 performances of the one-man show *Defending the Caveman*. He also coaches speakers. Kevin explained it to me this way:

> *Each time a presenter goes onstage, they are portraying a character, even if they are speaking as themselves, when they are speaking from a script. It's a slightly fictionalized version of the presenter.*

In other words, you have already scripted that eulogy or other emotion-laden speech. Like it or not, when you deliver it, you are displaying a fictionalized version of yourself: who you were when you first thought to write down those words. Every rendition of them from that point on is a portrayal. So, because you are "acting out" that scene anyway, why not use the best tools at your disposal? Now those tools include practice and emotional substitution. When used with integrity, they will allow you to deliver emotional content in an authentic way, while maintaining control instead of letting your emotions control you.

Don't look to your audience for therapy

Another of my wife's experiences illustrates a danger that you may encounter as a speaker. Again, a funeral was involved. This time, the deceased was the adult son of an older couple in our church. When my wife met with the family to plan the memorial service, the father insisted on being given a time to speak.

When that time came, the result was painful and awkward as the father rambled on for at least 15 minutes, clearly trying to process his grief over his son's unexpected and untimely death. There was nothing in the remarks that helped the gathered mourners to know his son better, to celebrate his life, or to come to terms with their own grief. It was all about the father. The audience was squirming in their seats long before he was done. My wife and I exchanged glances—but what could she do? (Since that experience, she has learned always to ask for *written* comments from any family member requesting to speak at a memorial service.)

The father did not approach that pulpit with any audience benefit in mind. His only thought was to unburden himself. That is an observation, not a criticism. At that point in his grief process, it was all that could have been expected of him. Still, as speakers, we must learn from his experience. Do not look to your audience for grief therapy.

One of my wife's seminary professors put it so succinctly: "You can speak from your scars, but not from your wounds."

There will be times when you will speak of events that were painful to you when they happened. The speech that took me in 2018 to the semifinals of the World Championship of Public Speaking® included a scene of me at age 13, watching my hearing aid get run over by a truck while I was at band camp. At the time it happened, it left me in tears as I pondered trying to navigate band camp with a severe hearing loss. But by the time I told that story, it was an old scar, not a fresh wound.

The father at that funeral, on the other hand, was speaking from wounds that were still bleeding.

What about you? Are the painful events of which you speak sufficiently removed from your current circumstances that you can keep those feelings at arm's length as you talk about them? If not, then perhaps they are fresh wounds. If you are still bleeding emotionally, you are not ready to speak of those events to an audience. Talk through them with a trusted counselor instead.

Use the power of laughter

Finally, as we are talking about emotional content in a speech, let us not forget the power of *positive* emotions. Especially, let us consider the power of laughter to give your listeners relief from the intense feelings of sadness or pain that may arise from our stories of difficulty. In short, take them on an emotional roller coaster, with both highs and lows.

My wife is now a pro at doing this in funerals. She has found that family and friends of the deceased, in the midst of their grief, treasure the opportunity to laugh as they recall fond memories. While they are sad that their loved one is gone, they chuckle over remembered foibles and mishaps.

Laughter is a release of emotional tension. It doesn't take a funeral to build emotional tension. No doubt you have stories that do that. So why not follow such a story with something incongruous that evokes laughter? Your audience will feel better, and you will, too.

For a couple of insights into uncovering the humor in your stories, be sure to read Chapter 6 of the first volume in this series, *The Speaker's Quick Guide to Telling Better Stories.*

There is a good chance you will someday speak at an emotionally charged event, or otherwise encounter highly emotional content in your speaking. By following the tips in this chapter, you will be better prepared to come across as both authentic and in control. The two are not mutually exclusive.

CHAPTER 7

Go for connection, not perfection

"All faults may be forgiven of him who has perfect candor."

—WALT WHITMAN

Consider where we've come in this journey together. From a starting point of finding the worthiness of your message, through focusing on your audience and practical techniques for managing nervousness, we have covered quite a bit of ground. My intent is for you to finish this book more confident than when you started—confident in the value of your message to others and in your ability to present it to them effectively, no matter who they may be.

But I would not want to leave you with the impression that your worth as a speaker depends on how effectively you overcome signs of nervousness like sweaty palms and a tight throat. On the contrary, the value you bring to an audience depends on one thing above all others: *your willingness to be vulnerable as you connect with them.* Therefore, I shall leave you with a few thoughts on vulnerability and connection.

Brené Brown says, "Vulnerability is the last thing I want you to see in me, but the first thing I look for in you."[1] In other words, to truly give our audience what they want from us as speakers, we must be prepared to shed our armor and show up as we truly are. And that's not easy.

I remember a time when I felt the most vulnerable in a public setting and was called upon to speak. It was six months and a day after my father had died in Texas, where I grew up. My family was gathered in North Carolina for my sister's wedding. My four-year-old, who couldn't understand how we could be celebrating a happy occasion without her grandfather there, was acting out. Aside from my immediate family, I was surrounded by many people I had never met before. And then my mother turned to me and said, "You know, you're going to have to offer a toast since your dad's not here."

I had maybe twenty minutes to think about it over the reception dinner. And then the Best Man got up and delivered a cringe-worthy toast, with uncomfortable references to the groom's divorce. With the audience thus warmed up, it was my turn.

"I want you to think about your family," I started. "There are only three ways a person comes into a family: birth, adoption, and marriage. Today, we celebrate [the groom] coming into our family…" and I took off from there. I wish someone had recorded it, because beyond that I cannot recall what I said. I just know that somehow, I worked in a reference to my late father, while making it an uplifting, though poignant, moment.

I'm sure I finished with something like, "Here's to the happy couple," along with a feeling of relief that I had simply gotten through it. It was the most vulnerable—and perhaps the least articulate—I had ever felt in front of an audience. And I remember my mother looking up at me from the next chair with a teary smile.

Later, the Maid of Honor told me, "David, when even the waiters are crying, you know you nailed it." Perhaps I did. I did not set out to "nail it." I set out to express the deep gratitude my family felt for those guests giving us the space to "feel all the feels," as my daughter likes to put it. I felt nervous and unprepared. And yet, in that moment, I allowed myself to be vulnerable. My words and my vulnerability connected with those wedding guests. Because even though most of them did not know me, they knew my sister. They knew she had been planning a wedding while grieving her father's death.

In effect, it was left to me to name the elephant in the room. How could we be so happy and sad at the same time? The four-year-old was not the only one struggling with that. Somehow, in my vulnerability, I managed to capture that contradiction. And in doing so, I gave permission to everyone there to live in that contradiction with us.

Ultimately, it was not my wordsmithing but my vulnerability that connected with that audience. Therefore, the thought I want to leave you with is simply this: *Go for connection, not perfection.*

Striving for perfection when speaking will lead inevitably to several undesirable outcomes:

- You will be "in your head," trying to remember the exact words and delivery you had planned, and in so doing you will miss the opportunity to connect emotionally with your audience.
- You will become even more nervous as you become aware of the gap between the speech you planned to give and the

speech you are giving.
- You will likely come across as stiff, wooden, and unrelatable.

By contrast, when you focus on *connecting* with your audience, you will come across as much more genuine and approachable. Not only that, but connecting emotionally also makes your content more memorable. In the words of Hall of Fame speaker Patricia Fripp, "People will not remember the words you say, but they will remember how they felt when they heard you say them."

Not only will they not remember your words, but they also will never know if the words they heard deviated in any way from the words you had in your head. So lay aside any thoughts of delivering a "perfect" speech; instead, strive for connection. That is the gift you will give your audience.

---

[1] Brown, op. cit., p. 113

Presenting with confidence to a virtual audience

As this book prepares to go to press, speakers everywhere are faced with an unprecedented shift from in-person to virtual appearances. The novel coronavirus pandemic is upsetting patterns of travel and commerce worldwide. Even once this is over, it seems likely that many such patterns will not return to pre-pandemic dimensions for quite some time. Therefore, it appears reasonable to assume that virtual speaking appearances will continue to be the rule rather than the exception. How does this shift affect the way you apply the lessons of this book? This Appendix provides some brief answers. For a more in-depth treatment, refer to the first of the Recommended Resources in the next section.

Chapters 1 and 2: Your message and your audience

The main points of these chapters are that your message deserves to be told, that you deserve to tell it, and that your focus should be on your audience and what you are there to do for them. These points are equally true when your audience is not in the same room as you. When you're speaking remotely, it remains important to consider your audience's needs first, and it ought not be any harder to do so. What may be harder in a remote situation is remaining convinced that your audience wants you to succeed when you cannot see them. Remember to focus on what is universal in your unique experience and how what you learned can help others.

Chapter 3: Preparation

Everything in Chapter 3 is equally applicable whether you are appearing in person or via a virtual speaking platform. However, you might consider the impact of presenting virtually on your internalization process. On the one hand, if you are sitting in front of a webcam, there is not much opportunity to incorporate movement across the stage. Therefore, movement as an aid to memorization may not be available to you. On the other hand, you may find less of a burden on you to internalize your content. Perhaps you can keep your script open on a monitor that is close enough to your webcam that you can glance at it with minimal loss of audience contact. In any case, you should practice speaking while looking into your camera, as this is the way your audience perceives you are making eye contact.

In some cases, you will be recording your content for later playback instead of delivering it in a live virtual setting. I recently contributed my content to a major scientific association in this way. Because the presentation was almost an hour long, I took advantage of the opportunity to record it using a Teleprompter. This is a device that reflects your script (from the screen of a tablet or other device) on a tilted glass in front of your camera lens, so that you can read the script while appearing to make eye contact with the camera and hence the viewer. A word of caution is in order: The ability to appear natural while doing so is not automatic. It takes practice to minimize the eye movements that give away the fact that you are scanning the text. When done well, it is a great alternative to memorizing a long presentation.

Finally, don't underestimate the power of a Toastmasters club to help you achieve comfort in a virtual setting. At the time of this writing, all of the clubs I know of are meeting virtually.

Chapter 4: Practical tips

The eight tips in Chapter 4 will help you calm your nerves whatever your delivery medium may be. In the case of virtual presentations, some may be more helpful than others. For
example, consider the 10-to-1 rule. The outward signs that you are nervous may be even less evident when you are presenting a limited view of yourself to your audience. On the other hand, if you are seated as you speak, breathing well may be even more of a challenge. If you must be seated, therefore, follow the advice of every choir director: sit tall on the front edge of your chair, with your feet flat on the floor. This is the best seated position where breathing is concerned.

And here are a few more tips that apply specifically to virtual presentations:

- Raise your camera to eye level.
- Check your lighting to ensure your face is well lit and your
  background is neither too dark nor over-lit.
- Ensure you have a clutter-free background.
- Avoid using your computer's built-in microphone if possible.
  Use a microphone that is closer to your mouth, by using
  either a good-quality headset or a USB microphone.
- Avoid facing the wall as you speak. Not only does this
  common error make lighting your face more challenging,
  but it also puts a psychological barrier between you and
  your audience. Arrange your space so you are facing into
  the room, and picture your audience there with you.
- If possible, use a second monitor, especially if you plan to
  incorporate screen-sharing into your presentation. Keeping
  track of everything on one monitor can be difficult and will
  leave you flustered.

Following these tips will help you appear more professional and feel more confident in your presentation.

Chapter 5: Presenting to a high-status audience

Everything in this chapter applies equally well to virtual presentations. Here is an additional tip: if you are going to incorporate visual aids, be sure you are well-practiced on the platform you will be using.[1] If you are screen-sharing, do not share the PowerPoint window and then start the slideshow; that is sloppy and unprofessional. Start the slideshow first and then share the slideshow, not the PPT window.[2] (Here is where having a second monitor is helpful.) When you go into screen-sharing mode, your first slide should be visible immediately. You should never have to ask, "Do you see my title slide?"

Chapter 6: Handling emotional content

Having seen my wife (the pastor) officiate at live-streamed funerals, I realize that almost any in-person event you can name must have a virtual counterpart as well.

Therefore, the same principles apply. Speak from your scars but not from your wounds. Practice those words that make you choke up until you can get through them. Allow emotion to come through but not to take over. And never forget the power of laughter to offset emotional tension.

While I may hope never to deliver a toast at a virtual wedding, who can say? Should that time come, be prepared!

Chapter 7: Connection vs. perfection

Vulnerability in front of a room full of strangers may be the second-hardest thing you will ever have to do as a speaker. Vulnerability in front of an unseen webinar audience will likely be the hardest. Yet, as Chapter 7 shows, that vulnerability is what allows the audience to connect with you at an emotional level so that your message can find a home in their hearts and minds.

Given the degree of control you may have over both your physical and your virtual environment (or platform) when you present remotely, it may be tempting to strive for a higher level of polish than you might achieve in an in-person speaking engagement. Try not to give in to this temptation. Yes, you want to appear professional and well-prepared. But if you do so at the expense of allowing yourself to be vulnerable, you will run headlong into the undesirable outcomes listed in Chapter 7: you will be "in your head" and unrelatable.

Therefore, focus on connection. Use your stories. Use the "and, but, therefore" structure described in Chapter 6. Use audience-centric language (lots of "you" and "your"), even when you can't see the audience. Follow Brené Brown's advice, drop the armor, and show up as you truly are. Engage with your audience by whatever means are available in your virtual platform: Q&A, chat, white boards. Let them see that you are still learning how to engage in this new, more virtual world, just as they are. Be approachable. Strive for connection above all else.

If this all sounds quite daunting, remember you are not alone. And there are resources available to help you, including the ones listed in the next section.

---

[1] For platform-specific help that is beyond the scope of this book, there are video tutorials available for

Zoom, Microsoft Teams, Adobe Connect, Google Meet, and just about any such program you can name.

[2] Windows users: become familiar with the Alt+Tab function. Mac users: Command+Tab.